Ana's Journey

A Brazilian Mother's Story of Kidnap, Forced Marriage and Her Botched Abortion

Ina Silva-Sobolewski
Ron Judah Friedman

Based on a true story

Dedication

To every woman who has ever faced the pain, humiliation, loneliness and despair of an unwanted pregnancy—and who had little or no support to bring her baby to term—and has lived with the regrets that come with terminating a new life...

To every abortion survivor who was delivered alive and well, in spite of the circumstances surrounding a mother's desperate decision. May all who have endured this emotional and psychological grief find solace and endure in newness of life...

Your pain is never far from our hearts...

And may your child's beating heart never be far from yours.

Prologue

My mother narrated to me (Ina)—when I was twelve—the basis of the story you are about to read.

She was so ashamed of what she called her "secret" that she asked me to keep quiet about it until she was gone from this world. Her story is one shared by millions of women worldwide: single women, married women, young and old, poor and rich, educated and uneducated, black and white, women from all walks of life. My mom, like these many women, felt compelled to abort her pregnancy.

My mother would not have looked back and shared this story had she no one to look to for forgiveness. But she had inside her, not just the seed of an unborn baby, a fetus she chose to abort, but she also had the seed of God's love that had been planted years before. She had not tilled that soil, as she should have, but my mother turned back to this loving God, who she knew would be her and her unborn child's only chance at redemption.

ೞറ೧ൠ

Nobel Peace Prize recipient, the late Agnes Gonxha Bojaxhiu, known by tens of millions as Mother Teresa of Calcutta, wrote that, "The poverty of being unwanted, unloved, uncared for is the most terrible poverty." Is there a woman alive who hasn't felt that kind of poverty at some time in her life? My mother Ana was no exception. At a time in her life when she had no money, credit card, saving bonds or someone to love, she found Joseph, with whom she would spend the rest of her life.

When she first met him, there was no intention of falling in love; after all she was focused solely on helping her family survive in the absence of the loving parents who had died a few years before. But the richness of Joseph's affections finally poured as a heap into the poverty of her lonely life. Thus, the path toward marriage began.

Ana's Journey

That path led to a joyous afternoon in the summer of 1961, during a typical steamy Brazilian summer, when Ana and Joseph finally—and mutually—consented to marriage. They had known each other for ten years. Theirs, they vowed, would be a union as sturdy as a Samaúma tree, rooted deep into the substratum of mutual respect. They resolved to build a stable layer of love anchored below the twisted and chaotic lives they had witnessed—lives which involved rampant, alcohol-enraged turmoil, the untimely deaths of two parents, and long stretches of poverty.

On the day Ana and Joseph wed, the ceremonial party was a simple affair; both the bride and groom came from humble backgrounds and had little money.

Joseph had left his family years before to venture into São Paulo alone: he was a young, uneducated *nordestino*; in other words, a rural redneck who came to a city of 17 million in hopes of making a better life.

That redneck was my father, his wife my mother, Ana. They were a young couple crushed by poverty that struggled, but stayed together.

༺༻

Their first baby was born just ten months after their wedding. The second one, a boy, was born eleven months later and six months after that Ana found herself pregnant again. This third pregnancy came as a problem, though, because Joseph had just lost his job in extremely bad economic conditions.

They thought abortion would be the sensible decision to make sure they didn't sink any deeper into poverty, like so many others they saw around them. They were living in desperate times and feared the dire challenges they would face if they let this new baby live.

It is often during a moment of desperation when one cannot see past the uncertain future. Ana and Joseph felt trapped. What else could they do to protect themselves and their family?

A permanent solution to a temporary problem seemed like the only way out.

In Ana's case, her desperation started long before she and Joseph ever met.

It had started on the day Ana's mom died, when she was only six years old. She found herself faced with the sorrow of a lonely life.

For Joseph, the decision to terminate a life—the life he helped create—came subconsciously. When he was eight, he had watched the pitiful wretch of his drunken father die in the middle of a muddy street.

He carried the weight of that memory with him all his life, much in the way Ana had suffered from the loss of her mother.

This is the human side of the Amazon's vine, the *liana*, twisting its tendrils across many hearts when a tiny seed that two had planted was almost destroyed … until the "master gardener" redeemed it.

❧☙

"Mamãe, wake up; wake up ... Papai fell in a puddle … he isn't moving."

The words stuck in his throat.

Joseph was eight when his father collapsed in the street, a pathway of dust turned to mud like many in 1940s Brazil.

When the rainy season comes in September, the downpour converts the dust of the unpaved roads into streets that shine like carnival slides for those who must carry themselves along the treacherous routes. The monsoons don't discriminate. A young child or a middle-aged man can drown in seconds as the unpaved roads change from arid canals to rain-soaked rapids.

Joseph saw his drunken father lose his footing and fall on his face in a puddle—of water no deeper than the rum sloshing in the bottle still held loosely in his right hand.

Pried free by the rains, the small bottle had sailed down the street, a glass urn holding the man's final rum-sweetened drops of spit—perverse "last rites" of a life devoted to drink. Too inebriated to even raise his head, Joseph's father died before his young boy's eyes. The man left his wife a widow and his children without a father.

Joseph's silent oath that noon was one he kept till the day he drew his final breath. The bottle would not own him the way it owned his father.

Still, the memory haunted him.

He felt helpless when thoughts of what had happened played in his head, but so began his forced manhood. Joseph stepped into his father's shoes and suddenly found himself in the position of head of a four-person household.

The task of providing for the family now fell on his unseasoned shoulders. The family consisted of his mom, Poli (short for Apolinaria), a sister two years younger, and a brother who was one year his junior. The hardships that Joseph endured weighed heavily on his mind years later, when, as a father of two, he would consent to terminate the third child his wife was preparing to carry to term.

༄༅

Joseph's tragedy hit him hard that day. But an even crueler downpour of grief, unknown to him, had watered the trunk of his family tree. For his grief, as bad as it had seemed, was merely a sliver of what had befallen Apolinaria, his mother, when she was just a few years older than him.

Like the god of the ancient myths that gave root to her real-life name, Apolinaria had shone as a supernal mortal of light, youth and beauty—with the same traits attributed to her namesake Apollo. A native from the Tucano tribe, Poli grew up in the northwestern part of the Amazon rainforest.

Unlike her mythical counterpart, this youthful Poli did not possess the attribute of prophecy. Had she been blessed with a prophetic gift, she would not have wandered into the dense forest, alone, defying her mother's repeated warnings. But the maturity of womanhood is lost on a "what does Mom know?" 13-year-old girl.

"Stay away from the black market whiskey sales," Poli's mother would tell her. "Those are men to be feared."

But Poli was young, with an adventurous spirit. She ignored the stark advice of her "overprotective" mother not to go toward certain parts of the rainforest. She and her friends walked ever deeper into the thicket of plants that Poli knew she could use to concoct her homemade cosmetics.

I will have the prettiest face paints of any of my friends! The allure of it led her further into danger. *Look at this plant! Nobody will have this one*, Poli thought. As she meandered through the maze of foliage, the chatter of her friends became distant whispers.

Poli and her friends had only weeks earlier become teens. The Quarup festival would be the chance for her and her friends to shine in the ceremonial spotlight, before their tribal leaders and elder kinsmen.

Poli and her friends had been rehearsing their dances for many days. The annual Quarup, a community-wide dance, memorial, and party involved a gathering of villagers to enjoy food and music while honoring their ancestors.

In memorializing the dead, they also honored the cycle of life, death and rebirth, which included as a central event the introduction of those girls who had reached their menarche. As soon as these girls experienced that first menstruation, they would be married off by their parents, in arranged, sanctioned partnerships.

At the Quarup, the girls were afforded their first opportunity to display, as women, their natural beauty——with the help of indigenous plant-derived extracts, such as heartwood, bloodwood or campeachy. This would be the first time for them to apply on their bodies and faces the organic pigments and powders they had crushed and crafted themselves: what we now call *makeup*.

With the newfound maturity of being female and thirteen, Poli felt confident enough to go into the forbidden forest area alone ... perhaps too confident. Poli, the proud, ambitious Amazonian, was unable to see how vulnerable she was.

Dreaming big, fanciful thoughts beneath the broad-veined, leafy trees, Poli came face-to-face with the brutal, tragic fist of fate.

"What are *you* doing here?" Poli's voice trembled with terror as she turned and saw a city man come toward her. His scraggly beard and stinky sweat turned him into an ugly beast.

"What are you doing? Let go of me!" But he was stronger. What could she do?

"Let *go*! Help me ... Mommm ... ma ... Mo– ... mmmmm!"

Her screams went unheard.

The hellish hand of fate closed around her mouth. The man was not worried that Poli's momma would hear her screams. He knew no one would come to her rescue this day. He clamped his sweat and rum-stained fingers against her dry, trembling lips, for that hand had now become a granite seal that affixed its drop of hardened wax upon her destiny.

Poli's inner goddess light, composed of youth and beauty, was evident to this base, demented man. And not a dewdrop of empathy or affection formed in his barren soul. This was where the story of the delighted gods parted from the ways of the debased world.

As she stepped into the forest that day, when her innocence and love of life streamed from her like sunny rays shining through campeachy branches, Poli dreamed of her wedding day.

Ah, what a sweet moment, she imagined...

I will put a tiara of orchids and twisted heartwood twigs on my head and finally fill out my beautiful wedding outfit.

That fantasy of being matched with a husband died on the rainforest floor. The three days of celebration that would have followed turned into three days of torment. Poli's first trip outside the forest led to years of entrapment.

Poli couldn't flee. The man had kidnapped her and made sure his prey couldn't get far. By the time he got to the river to take a taxi boat, it was dark. Her capture ran its course for several days ... the mismatched couple stuffed like smelly fish on the boat, the two of them enduring long rides on trains and buses, and their arrival when her assailant finally brought her to a town on the outskirts of a place she later learned was Salvador, located along the southwestern tip of Brazil.

Poli's ability to speak three tribal languages did not help her. With more than 180 languages and dozens more dialects used among the many native tribes of the rainforest inhabitants, the language barrier proved too high a hurdle for Poli to overcome.

"Me ajude por favor," she would say. *Help me please.* "Minha família está me procurando." *My family is looking for me.*

But her words dropped like globs of wood pulp squashed beneath her feet.

She tried many times to fashion her silly pleas into stronger communicative strands, but what were meant as lifelines to secure her freedom proved no more than twisted vines of gibberish that her fellow Indian tribesmen could not grasp. Her abductor spoke for her wherever they went. His lies were *lianas* (rainforest vines) that tightened his grip around her, choking off the joy she once knew. Her requests begging for help went unanswered, in the same way as her nightly cries to her faraway mom, and her home village's spirits and trees.

The house he brought her to smelled and looked worse than a pigsty. Poli hated everything about her counterfeit husband and the place he had brought her to. She was a caged parakeet.

Poli tried many times to claw her way out of her lonesome coop, but was stopped every time. Even after she'd walked for hours toward a path home, she was too young, too poor, too tired, and too naive to escape a city that now closed in around her. There were no alerts about lost children in 1930s' Brazil, and in a big city like Bahia, people could not pick up a phone to call the police. Poli had no wings to flap for the sky and leave for good.

The fire in her eye, her soul, and her heart was not enough to gain her freedom. She could only crawl back like a dumb hen for the food she needed to stay alive, knowing the trade-off would be the continued rapes. To venture too far from this "homestead" could possibly put her in even greater dangers.

Then, a month or so after another of the monster's rum-induced "trysts," Poli discovered she was pregnant. This girl who had been a virgin, had now, over several months, seemed to age ten years—but a year after being stolen from her home, she would soon become a mother to the child she had not planned to bear. *And who knows*, Poli thought, *this little person inside of me could one day help me return home to the rainforest.* Slowly Poli accepted the fact that this dubious new life was now *her* new life—no matter how hard she fought emotionally against it.

Though it was nothing like the planned pregnancy for which she once yearned, this fresh-faced, needy baby helped her confront her situation with awakened optimism. The fire-eyed seed growing inside her helped Poli anchor herself to more solid ground. Now she had someone to call her own, someone to love and to teach her language to, someone to share her dreams with and tell jungle stories to. Together, she and her child, they would struggle under this despot and his tyranny.

In ten years, at twenty-three, Poli would have three children. Joseph was her oldest. The father of these children continued to mistreat her and them and withheld money she needed for clothes and food. He made her beg for everything.

Though she was too reserved and dignified to knock on neighbors' doors for giveaways, Poli's neighbors noticed her dire circumstances and would offer their hand-me-downs and leftovers, which she graciously accepted.

The children rooted her. Gardening helped her flourish, to nurture bigger dreams of freedom. The collards, cassavas, beets and beans she grew raised the stakes for her and her children. Poli knew by tilling the land that she was tilling their future.

This future would one day lead to a harvest that her children could reap. She aspired for a better life; this meant Poli would have to—for now—bury any hopes of escape.

Her husband's monthly trips to sell black-market rum turned their home into madness upon his return. He came back drunk from these trips and poured out his ill will toward his wife and kids as plentifully as he poured out the rum into his twisted face.

He had been addicted to alcohol for so long by this point that he was downing about one entire 750 mL bottle a day by the time he died.

After her husband's death, Poli wanted to return to family, but scarce resources kept her from doing more than considering the journey. *I barely have money to buy food for my kids*, she thought. *How can I pack us across a country to find parents that may no longer be alive?*

As a mother, Poli knew her kids better than they knew themselves and she understood the very real possibility that they would rebel—that they would hate their new home in the forest, having known only city and village life. It would be far from a sure thing that they would welcome a "return" to a simple, isolated life they had never known. She was right to worry that they would see this uprooting as an unbearable burden.

Her children's escape would be a relief for Poli, the girl whose last memory in freedom was of happily picking flowers for the community-wide gathering.

The more she sifted reality from the dream, the clearer Poli could see her future, and her vision for improving her children's lives. Getting them used to working hard to better their lot was crucial.

Joseph quit school and got a job on a farm to help the family survive. By age ten, he was driving

400-horse-power tractors and would eventually go on to drive open-bed produce trucks that brought in the bulk of the money to support the family. Although for his age he had suffered a lot, Joseph was a happy, responsible kid.

His mom always encouraged him and the other children; she gave them love, attention and hope for a brighter, more promising future. Almost every night after dinner the kids and their mom would sit outside their little house and she would look at the nighttime moon and stars. She told them how to forecast the next day's weather. She told them stories from the rainforest and answered their questions with other stories, stories she kept in her head like packets of seeds she sprinkled to make life better with memories. Some stories she told scared them, but others made them laugh.

Joseph stared at his mom while she was caught up in telling her stories. *She's so young and has been through so much in her life,* he thought. *Yet how loved and protected she's always made us feel.*

Poli, who was young in years but wise like a woman of ninety, was very protective of her kids. As she told another forest tale with the stars sprinkling their shine from a million miles away, she couldn't stop thinking; *I don't* ever *want them to go through what I've been through.*

When her teenage son told Poli about job opportunities in São Paulo, almost a thousand miles away, she was glad for him, but sad too. Leaving for

São Paulo would be a godsend, for she'd heard that anyone making the venture there would find work.

Manufacturing in 1937 Brazil had become the mainstay of mercantile production after the two-year-long drought in the north decimated the livestock. The people had fled to São Paulo like locusts.

As a highly skilled truck driver, Joseph could take a top-paying blue-collar job. Yet the money he promised to send would take very good care of her two other children and allow her to purchase a nicer house. He vowed he'd visit every year. When he went to his mom to tell her, she hesitated, then gave the blessing he knew she would. But her eyes expressed the words her mouth could not—that seeing him leave would be another anguish she would have to endure.

Only a mother knows the folly of a well-intentioned promise.

❧

He boarded a *pau de arara*, or "parrot's perch," a type of flatbed, open-air truck to which were erected poles for passengers to hold, similar to the way parrots were sold in the market. Joseph and his fellow passengers sat on their bags or held tightly to the wooden poles that framed the truck as it pounded the unpaved pothole-strewn roads. There were nursing mothers, sniffling kids, sick older men —plus a bevy of dogs, chickens and cats.

The people rolled and heaved, sweated and endured, as did the truck that ferried them from their drought-stricken "Egypt" onto the path that held so much promise. Their course spiraled up and over and around the sere hills leading them into São Paulo.

Before Joseph began his journey, he faced the forlorn look of love mixed with despair as Poli (and Joseph's siblings) stood watching him leave. Poli and Joseph both knew instinctively that this passage of his would bring epochal changes. All they could do was the very thing Poli had taught them these many years: hope and work for a better tomorrow. And with that whisper of a shared thought, Joseph and his mother managed a last look at each other's more-distant face ... now made invisible by clouds of red dust.

As the hundred-degree heat swarmed his eyes and hair, and his skin tingled with *pernilongo* stings (*Brazilian mosquito*), Joseph knew his loving mom could do nothing to protect him now. The trip took several days, but Joseph's eyes brimmed with hope despite the swirling dust and steam.

Most of the men had left their wives and children behind with the expectation of returning soon. Joseph left with no such expectation. Instead, he left a chunk of his heart behind in the only home he had known.

What if I can't get a job? What if I run out of money? What if I don't find a place? These fears weighed on Joseph's mind, but he was not alone in this.

The men knew that a fantasy of the unknown was unlikely to match the reality of the known. Life's uncertainties were real, but Joseph's desire to succeed was more real. Finally, after what seemed like forty days, he arrived at the big, bright city carrying a heavy bag and a heavier heart.

He was not prepared for the city that awaited him. Here, life zipped by at the clip of a freight train and if he couldn't keep up that train would run right over him. And no one would care. There wasn't time to talk or sit, eat dinner or sit outside with family or friends, no special moments to stare at the moon or stars.

Joseph quickly found a good room at a boarding house. Magdalena was the landlord, a pretty blonde with soft green eyes, and she gave two meals a day with the rent. Her husband helped to maintain the boarding house and care for their developmentally disabled son. After Joseph and Magdalena became friends she confided to him of her two previous abortions. That was Joseph's first time hearing about abortion. *Abortion? What is that? You mean a woman could stop the baby growing inside her ... Just like that?*

He had never heard of such a thing.

He was a good man who grew up listening to his mom and never once questioned her inviolable love for him, or his siblings. For that reason, some perceived Joseph as simple-minded. But the fact was, people liked him. He was a patient, well-groomed young man and was seen as a very decent guy who had a good heart. When Magdalena confided to Joseph her regrets, he wondered along with her, what her two unborn babies would have looked like. Then, as she sipped her tea, he saw a big drop fall into her cup. And he could see how heavy the burden must have been to carry that regret all these years. Little did he anticipate, years later, that he would make the same tragic decision.

He found a job right away. Joseph was a very good truck driver and though he was only seventeen and without a driver's license, he was able to land a position with a small transportation company. He worked fourteen-hour days, making twice as much as his job back home had paid.

After months learning to navigate the roads that cut across this huge, now-familiar city, Joseph got an opportunity to drive a city bus. This allowed him to wear a clean, ironed uniform to work and make even more money. By now, Joseph had been living in São Paulo for three years, still at Magdalena and her husband Renato's boarding house. Joseph would send money to Mamãe every month, as promised; but the busy, nonstop life of São Paulo had kept him tied to his new home. Despite the promise, he had not visited his mother even once. His job demanded he stay in the city to work. Vacations were luxuries he could not afford. Thinking that all of the pieces would fall into place was the fantasy that filled his head on the truck ride to São Paulo. In fact it would be another *twenty years* before he'd wrap his arms around his mother's shoulders, his own wet with her tears.

The two exchanged letters every week since he arrived in São Paulo, though. He sent pictures, updated her on his goings-on, and enclosed enough réis (then the currency) to know that his small packages would help take the sting out of her and his siblings' situation.

Poli could not read or write, but with the money Joseph sent, his brother and sister could now go to school instead of working on the farm all day like he had to do. Despite his solitude he knew his love reached them like a mile-long liana rooting him to his family.

He couldn't deny that his life in the big city brought isolation and moments of despair. The serene, happy stargazing sessions with his mom and the kids was now a dry sapling stuck into a basin of gravelly dirt. His urban, blue-collar routine consisted of going to work, going home after work, eating, sleeping and doing it all again day after day. When the weekend came, he went to the weekly dance, where he shook off loneliness that clung to him like a coat of thorns.

He met a cavalcade of girls, lonely and far from home like him, but their many trinkets and charms failed to seduce him. He was looking for an authentic oasis of love, the girl who would stay the course and steer him on that path of mutual respect, affection and steadfastness. He was, without thinking so, looking for an image of his mother in a girl to call his own.

While at work, in what had become a monotonous and dreary landscape of a city bus route, he spotted his fountain spouting beauty and youth. Ana would quench his thirst and slake his desire—with her clear, cool canteen of commitment. She was everything he wanted and a little bit more. For Ana was as beautiful a young woman as he had seen. And he had seen many. It was the things of God to come, that he had not seen, that would alter his sense of destiny from then on.

૱ଔ

Ana hailed from Bahia state, and had come to São Paulo the same way as Joseph. Ana's father and mother were two solid branches of the same tree and had grown very happy together over the years. Unlike Joseph's father, Ana's father had no drinking problems and he loved and respected his wife and children.

    A crazed man had not forcibly taken Ana's mom as a girl, but her mother knew the pain of being made an emotional hostage. For her mom's family had deserted her. Her parents dreamed of her marriage to a rich Portuguese man that lived near, but she crushed their hopes and instead married a young mulatto farmer. He was seventeen; she was sixteen. They met and got married within a year. Although she left the rich life filled with servants and weekend parties, she quickly latched onto her husband's simpler world, and stepped onto the working-class path. Initially she missed her parents, but content with a man she loved and who she knew loved her, she gladly fell into the role of nurturing mother once the babies came. First came a son, and then followed five boys and three girls.

Ana's mom had served as the perfect role model for Ana of what a loving mom was meant to be. Her face was constantly at the ready with a warm smile and her arms seemed always reaching down to hug one of the kids that clamored for her attention.

She was only six, but remembered the morning her mom told them of a new sibling who would be coming into their family. It was another wondrous and sunny day deep in the north of Brazil—and early—when her dad skirted off in a rush, and returned hours later with two stern-faced women.

At certain times, usually during moments when he was exceptionally playful or perturbed, Ana's dad called her by a pet name, Nana.

Nana, these ladies are here to help get the baby from Mamãe's tummy.

Inside, the parents tended their room meticulously, neat, with linens spread like ripples of clean water they unfolded on the white bed with a sheet that hung from a pole stretched across the wall. But when she craned her neck to look, Ana saw that her mother's tawny face had turned a shade of opaque white she had never seen.

Nana, wait outside! Her father barked an order that she instantly obeyed.

As she left, her small eyes glanced up at the towering women. Their granite faces held cold, carved expressions. Her child's mind, just a piece of soft chalk, was no match to scratch the surface of that rock-hard look.

She went to her room and laid down on her bed. As she fell asleep she pictured a huge ghost like thunder that roared beside her six-year-old's ears. When Ana awoke to her mother's screams, she stiffened, then nervously exhaled as she heard a baby cry. Shuffling closer toward the women, who smiled and invited the kids to come and see the family's new addition. It was predawn, so they merely glimpsed the mucous-covered baby, kissed their mom and went back to bed. Mom looked tired and paler than the dry season's *caatinga* (white vegetation). It was a beautiful morning and the sun labored to stay alive another day. The sheets on the bed and walls still glistened white, but Ana perceived strains of gloom too. The sense of a morbid presence hid in a stark corner of the now decrepit room. And this barely breathing shadow, like a cat, waited to spring on an injured bird.

Her dad gladly cooked them fresh eggs, baked sweet potatoes and lovingly prepared a succulent cassava cake from *Mamãe*'s special recipe. After they ate, they surrounded their mom's bed and the new baby boy, who suckled at his mother's breast for his first post-pregnancy meal. Anna thought her mom's speech seemed slurred and her wan complexion signaled something wrong. Her mom's words stayed stuck in her mouth, but she lifted herself from her bed to check that her kids had eaten.

For two days, she at times sat up but did not leave her bed. She did not talk and could not even hold her baby to her breast. This time when her dad left for the two tall ladies they carried a large bucket and clean rags bunched in a loose ball that reeked with some foul-smelling salve.

This time the women's faces wore a plaster shroud etched with preoccupation and sorrow. After insulating her clammy arms and legs with the mold-smelling cloths, Ana's mom lay there as though laid out on a marble table. After the women left, Ana's dad was left alone—an anxious sentry guarding an indefensible tomb. How was this weakened and desperate man supposed to parent nine children by himself?

After breakfast on the third day, Ana ran to her mother's bedroom. She extended her finger and touched her mother's still-feverish forehead; it felt cold and wet with dried sweat. Their eyes met and Ana raised an arm to stroke her mother's long, straight hair. Cassava cake crumbs left a jagged line along the silky strands. A dim smile formed, but no words.

The two peered at the baby clutching the breast. Ana waited for her mom to say something, to share a new forest story, to ask her opinion for the baby's name ... or the hand-sewn dolls ... the animals born in the woods ... but there was a void where conversation should have been. As if her world now ran in slow motion ... Ana looked up to see her mom's eyelashes flicker. The eyes that seemed to long for other things, hallowed things that Ana couldn't see. Then, in unison, the tired eyelids closed. The orbs beneath–eyes that forever sparkled–now dimmed for a last time.

The baby's milky spittle pooled at the nipple of a breast that no longer heaved under the engine of breath.

Papa, Mamãe fell asleep with the baby!

Papa came running, quickly gave Ana the baby, and told her to leave. Ana heard him talk to her, softly at first, then louder. When he started to moan, cry, then wail, Ana knew. The sun inside had dropped from their sky.

After what seemed like hours, Ana's dad pulled open the door.

Their whispered thoughts and prayers echoed on: *Crianças, venham se despedir de sua mãe. (Children, come here and say goodbye to your mama.)*

He called the nine kids into the room to tell them their mom was gone. The next day their father explained that she had died of "an affection." A week later their newborn brother also died of "an affection" and the kids started crying. They worried they would all die soon because of the *affection* they had for each other. They had not known that affection could kill.

They remembered mama gently scolding them, *Não briguem; devemos demonstrar afeição! (Don't fight; we should show affection!)*

When their father saw them cry and heard them use the word *affection* instead of *infection*, he realized the mistake and consoled them, explaining that an "infection" had killed their mother and brother, *not an a-ffection.*

After the two deaths, and burials nearby, darkness blanketed the house. The family's former optimism settled like a dirty rag upon their hearts. Antonio, who wore his grief like a cloak pulled up around his shoulders, fought his incessant thoughts of emptiness and feelings of failure.

The downpour of the summer storms awakened in them a sense that the river of life, though dammed up by death, had burst through to carry them forward. They were headed toward an unknown future, one with washed-out trails and hidden curves around which they could not see.

Here were nine kids and a widower husband emptied of the life that had kept them going. The man who saw himself first as a husband was forced to see himself as the sole parent to his half-orphaned flock of children. The farm seemed a landlocked island of desolation. Yet it was a place that held all the provisions needed to nurture and be nurtured.

The grange's grandeur, with its open green pastures, fruit trees and well-fed birds cut through the dark clouds that had reigned over them. Oxen, cows, sheep, chickens and bulky waves of cassavas filled the plantation entrusted to them. The teeming forms of life served as spiritual clouds that fed their soul and let them rethink the reckless role that death had held.

This half-sized army of harvesters, the children, now jumped into action. Cultivating plant and animal life distracted the family from their sorrows and worries. The kids and their father realized that the aspects of the woman they had lost still lived on: her influential love, kindness and mercy carried through their hands.

The same germinating seed of life they helped till to fruition in the animals and stalks encircling them had been alive in her too. Loving *them* was her life. And loving her had never died. If anything, now that she was gone, their love for her had grown, like the dormant seeds they had planted months before.

Nature became their surrogate mom. The work was a way to give back to the land, to nurture it and nourish life from it. Nature was a different kind of mother, who at day's end would prod her earthbound kids to escape, gently calling to them, "Run to the river!"

They would jump in, letting the cool waters rinse the drudgery from their muscled limbs. The kids looked forward to the ritual of a daily bath in the stream. Every evening was a baptism that brought back happy memories—thoughts of when Mamãe used to lead them to the banks of the river to scrub dirty dishes and clothes, and all the while she watched them splash, swim and fish.

At the water's edge, Ana bent toward the ripples to look at the wet hair frame her face. She saw and heard Mamãe.

You are with me, my Love, wherever I go ... As I go with you.

See how this river bridges its banks? So my heavenly joy joins us.

The song was a meditation, a moving, liquid memory that Ana wanted to hold forever.

After the death, bathing in the river became her daily cure, her salve.

And the labor the children provided became their father's salve. Without them, and their cooperative care for each other, he doubted he would have lasted long alone. In the days and weeks after the loss, he would suffer episodes of despair so deep that he would let himself slide to the floor, in a stupor of sadness, where encircled by his kids he would sit and cry himself to sleep. He mulled over the morsels of memories that came when he thought deeply of his wife, but on these occasional days of intense brooding his stomach went empty. He lacked the desire to fill his mouth with food when his heart felt so full of love for the woman no longer alive in the flesh.

But for every moment that he felt despair, there was a moment when his kids reminded him of her. For them, he promised himself he would—and must—survive.

He found hope in the small things: daily chores, meals together, and the everyday interactions that kept their hearts hopeful. The cassava had to be converted into flour for him to sell. The flour was used to make tapioca starch, cakes, porridge and bags of culinary treats to be sold at the market.

The children quickly learned to respect, help and nurture; they became, each in their own way, a younger sibling's parent. The older ones left the house before dawn to tend the farm and returned well past when the sun had set. Their father traveled for days at a time to sell the harvested products. Five of the kids served as unofficial housewives cleaning, cooking, doing laundry and completing every chore that needed to be done. This routine of work transformed them from the cheerful kids of playful chatter to the task-oriented, responsible children they had become. Many sad, hard days weighed on them but they did what they could to have fun.

Often the littlest cried for his mom. At two, he didn't have a clue about death, and merely thought his mom was gone on a long trip like his dad had been so many times before. Even after he witnessed his dad's return, he'd always wait for hers.

Their father, a devout Catholic, made them recite the rosary every single day. It used to take such a long time that they started the recitation on the way to the river and continued it all through their bath. They usually finished the rote benedictions by the time they returned home from the river.

Taking advantage of the fact their dad no longer had a wife to keep them in line, the children instituted their own rules, which included conducting the mandated prayers while kicking around a homemade ball, bathing in the river, and walking to and from spots on the farm and areas nearby. Praying the rosary became so much a habituated activity that they didn't even know why they were praying while they prayed, but knew there would be tragic consequences for them should their dad discover they had not said the prayers.

Without their mom, the children became even closer to each other than they had been. It was the kind of closeness that survivors from a wrecked ship find themselves invested in: clinging to cracked crates of wood or preservers to stay alive, alone in a vast sea except for one object, a life raft. When a child was sick, the rest would collaborate and take turns comforting each other by sleeping beside the sick one, making tea and so forth. They were each other's life preserver.

One day, a younger brother of Ana woke up very hot; he wanted to stay in bed and complained every two minutes that the house was too cold.

"*Can I have some of that water?*" His voice sounded raspy and dry. *Water the cold ... it's too cold for the bird ... I want the water for me ... bring it to him now! ... It will be too cold for me.* The others responded generously, as their mother would have responded.

But his haunting mumbling incoherence reminded them of their mom's last murmurs, that morning before she died. With their dad gone on a business trip, they didn't know what to do, so Ana made an herbal tea remedy their dad had in days past prepared and given them for stomachaches.

The enfeebled boy drank the bland mixture for three days and three nights. Finally, on a Sunday morning the fever finally rolled off of him—a huge stone that had locked him in delirium, but now disappeared for him to breathe anew.

Their dad arrived home from his sales trip just in time to save the boy's life, but could do nothing to reverse the horrible epileptic fits that seized him the rest of his days.

That first year without their mom was the hardest. Corn stalks, cassavas, squash and sweet potatoes crammed acres of fertile land, surrounding a house barren of its mother to tend to her nine kids. No neighbors dared venture into this suffocating familial underbrush. Besides, one needn't dig too deep a well to hit a vein of insolvency that ran through every farm.

The infancy of drought had quickly learned to crawl and kick every rural farmer in the gut. Its impact killed his cattle and decimated his plantation. In the farmers' bare-bones, hardscrabble existence, priorities changed fast. The children soon left school and ceased to celebrate Christmas or birthdays, holidays or weekends. Their everyday life fell into a steady cycle of work, eat and live: in other words … survive or die.

Without electricity and conveniences like radio and TV, the family found happiness and substance in their lives by relying on each other to make ends meet. The gas lantern provided the children's only nightly light, a dismal substitute for a mother's goodnight kiss. By the glow of that light, the smaller kids fashioned dolls, balls and wood toys from whatever scraps they salvaged that afternoon. They shared with each other, finding ways to carry on.

༄༅༄

More than a year had passed since Ana's mom died. Keeping the house clean proved impossible for the father, though the children did their best. The one chore he managed was to keep his composure, warding off emotional duress and daily, visible stress.

His sullen face hinted at an even deeper grief. But this grief did not deter him from being a calming and gentle father who shaped his children's perspective by comforting and teaching them whatever affirming lessons he could. It was evident that all of them shared the pain of losing a loved one, but he had lost more than just a loved one; he had lost his first and only true love—a soul mate. Even twelve months later, he sorely missed a private, extended opportunity to grieve … a moment to mourn the sweeter half of his divided self.

After losing contact with his wife's parents, there was no way for him to notify them that their daughter had died. His parents had died years before, so he was left with no one from either family to help him. It bothered him that his kids had become *analfabetos*, or illiterates. He was forced to take the children from school because the family survival depended on them working.

One day the kids witnessed a perky woman come through their door along with their tired-looking dad and two small boys. *Is that an auntie? Is she one of mama's cousins from the far south of the country?* they wondered.

The children were surprised and uncertain about these new visitors, especially the woman. Arcanja was her name.

The way Ana's father met Arcanja, who would soon become his second wife, could have come right from the pages of an old-time fairy tale. An uneventful morning quickly turned to chaos as the rigorous quiet was broken by the gut-wrenching screams of a woman.

Someone is being murdered! thought Ana's dad, as he dropped everything and ran toward the screams. After the hundred-meter or so sprint, he came over a slight ridge to behold what seemed at first a mirage. There stood a diminutive woman, a living faerie, with wondrously long, shadowy curls. A long grey dress that curved up and around her shapely legs and waist blew in the light breeze.

Within seconds, the man took this scene in before interrupted by her ungodly shrieks. *Este maldito coisa está me matando! (This damn thing is killing me!) ... Ele está subindo na minha perna! (He's climbing up my legs!)*

She bleated into the sky as if calling Zeus to crash from the clouds to save her. One could say that her imaginary Zeus did come, if a weary peasant named Senhor Antonio could stand in as his replacement.

Senhor Antonio, Ana's chivalrous dad, did not understand immediately what was happening. No abusive man gripping a butcher's knife stood over the woman. No screeching vultures hacked at her head with beak or talons. No wolves tore at her tender flesh. And yet she stood screaming at the top of her lungs pointing one hand to the sky, and another set of fingers slapping at the bump inside her dress that bounced against her hand.

And then Senhor Antonio heard it.

reeebBIT ... reEEBbbiit!

Ah, Senhor Antonio mused, *it is a stupid frog.*

Her voice continued to shout.

Get it OFF me, GET the "sapo boy" (bullfrog) OFF ME!

Quickly, he scooped his big hands under the frantic female's long dress, cupped her calf, then knee, then her upper leg, then her lower thigh—even further until he instinctively pulled away. But then he felt his "maiden in distress" tug at his shirt as if to tell him to keep doing what he was doing. With one last intimate reach, he clasped his hands around the bulbous toad that had suctioned its way up her legs and yanked the slimy amphibian from its indecent nest.

Once her dress was patted down and he had turned his back so she could wipe the sliminess from her legs, Arcanja and Antonio walked, talking incessantly about what had happened. She blushed often as she recounted the start of her misadventure, but before too long her embarrassed retelling of the incident had constructed a cohesive bond between them.

The unique and unexpected circumstances of their meeting had now made them fast friends. As they strolled back toward his home, Antonio continued to ask thoughtful, probing questions that revealed there were parts of Arcanja that Antonio had yet to touch, and ways of knowing her that he yearned to learn.

"Boy, fetch some water!" he called to one of his sons as they entered the yard.

She explained that she had been taking a bus to a nearby city and had stupidly gotten off the bus one stop too soon. She decided to walk because another bus wouldn't come for twenty-four hours. He invited her over for some food and rest and their friendship blossomed quickly. Arcanja was a single mom, never married, with two boys from two different fathers, which in the 1940s qualified her as a woman of extremely poor repute. Desperate to find someone to marry and remove this stain from her reputation, Arcanja considered how a very unfairy-tale-like frog might have brought her to her unadorned prince.

Antonio was heir to a kingdom of nine motherless children; therefore, marrying Arcanja would be for him like solidifying his control over vast stretches of new territory by taking as his bride a powerful duke's prized daughter. What had merely been a stopover for coffee before the drenching rains, had, after them, turned into an overnight stay that became a weeklong retreat. She felt bad for him and his situation and decided to stay long enough to help clean the house—a suitable arrangement considering the lengths he had gone to help her.

Once reality set in after the fairytale-like week together, Arcanja and Antonio could see that she needed a place to stay and he needed a woman to take care of the house and kids. After a month on the ranch and feeling like an unappreciated Cinderella, with straw slippers instead of glass ones on her feet, Arcanja walked with Antonio up the steps of the only Catholic church in town.

Inside the red brick and mortar sanctuary, the spiraling pace of the fairy tale beginning of their meeting would soon unwind. As it turned out, Arcanja was as far removed from living up to her name (which meant *archangel*) as that frog climbing her legs was from being crowned a real-life prince. The wedding bells tolled as the two exchanged vows, but the tolling bells could not foretell how quickly and miserably the couple's connubial kingdom would crumble.

Instead of playing the part of an exuberant Brazilian princess, Arcanja had stepped into her evil stepmother's shoes. She showed no empathy at all, rather this anti-Cinderella treated her new "prince's" nine kids worse than stranded cats in the streets of Shanghai.

Ana's stepmom was always angry with her and her eight siblings, but provided an emotional cocoon of love and protection around her own two boys. Her daily entertainment seemed to be hitting her husband's kids for pretty much any infraction she could think of. *Ana, você deixou o vidro aberto? foi você? (Ana? Did you leave the jar unsealed? Did you!)*

Her hard hand came down so fast it seemed as if Ana's face was struck by a lightning bolt. Ana would carry that heavy red welt over her left eye to her grave.

No one knew where the anger came from, perhaps Arcanja had unconsciously fashioned her hand and heart into supple repositories of frustration. Regardless of the source, the family suffered as she retaliated against innocents for her own string of broken relationships.

Arcanja knew when she married Antonio that she would have nine more kids to mother, but perhaps the misery of her actually taking care of them proved too much for her. Not even thirty and a single mother of two, she suddenly became—during her husband's frequent absences—the sole teacher, physician, seamstress, cook, bather, gatherer, disciplinarian to eleven children desperate for her love and kind attention. Her unresolved loneliness might have been bearable had she had her husband's burly shoulder to occasionally cry on. Without that, the utter solitude of her desperation most certainly gave rise to her incessant yelling.

Her boys, safe from the brunt of her hostility, always ate first when their mother cooked. Besides being well fed, they also wore the cleanest, nicest clothes. It would be no surprise later, when Ana reached a low point in her life as wife and mother, that she would deflate the value of a life. Hadn't she lived that kind of life herself ... being continually deprived of a mother's encouragement, esteem and interest?

Arcanja certainly knew no life was perfect. Her own was a picture of failure and limitation. Hadn't she gotten stuck in an "unfortunate" situation? It was bad enough when she bore her first son outside of wedlock. After the second boy came (from another man who was not her husband), the talking behind her back and the embarrassment she caused her family increased tenfold.

The abandonment and ostracism she felt from family and neighbors led to her decision to leave her childhood village. That departure had brought her to the chance encounter with a frog and subsequently her unassuming prince.

With little maternal concern, Arcanja attended to the thankless task of teaching her husband's kids. With her own children, she spent much time and energy; with the others, she swept them along their school lessons in the same way she taught them to sweep the inside of their hay-mortared hut. This replacement to the loving mom they lost seemed a poor replica to the masterpiece their mother had been; but Ana and the kids could do nothing. They were thankful they were still all together.

When Ana's oldest brother Frank turned fifteen, he left for São Paulo, Brazil's largest city. There, like thousands of others his age, he searched for a better life, one that would offer him a job and a chance to go to school. He had promised the others that he would send for them once he got settled and saved enough of his earnings.

After two years, Ana's brother had set aside enough savings to send for them. His letter arrived telling them he had gotten a good job and had rented a big house. He sent enough money for them to buy tickets on the parrot's perch, or *pau de arara*, as it was called.

This was the most common mode of travel for thousands of Brazilians coming into São Paulo seeking work. By 1936, thousands more had come to escape the plague of the drought that covered the nine northern states. The dreaded decay—along with the pestilential spread of foot and mouth disease—led to massive crop failures and livestock deaths that resulted in the loss of a half million lives. It was under these conditions that the tickets for truck transit had arrived. With those tabs of parchment in hand, Senhor Antonio, his wife Arcanja, and their eleven children gratefully boarded their jittery perches on a gloomy day in June.

They had packed all they owned in anticipation of the five-day journey to the city. On that truck, the passengers took in the smells and sights of the overcrowded mass of humanity mixed with caged fowl, dogs and crated parrots, knowing their fate would soon be following its own pecking order among the millions venturing into São Paulo for jobs. After the ardors of the trip, the truck descended from the mountain and lumbered on another hour when finally the battered truck rolled to a stop. Ana, with others, enjoyed their advent into the new city, their cheeks marked tears mixed with the ruddy dust of their new home.

As they looked around for Ana's older brother Frank, she saw a man near the little store as passengers disembarked. She was surprised to see how much her brother, this man, had changed.

My goodness! Is that Frank? How old, how mature he looks ... nothing like the boy he was when he left us.

A tall, slim man with olive skin stepped toward them and as Ana's initial surprise turned to acceptance, and she ran to him, glad he had stayed true to his promise. She threw her arms about his chest as if to secure an extension of his trustworthiness. (She had heard from others in the village of men who forgot their families and turned to drink or girls once the city's wild side lured them from their responsibilities.) They hugged each other and cried for a long time before finally loading into the station-wagon taxi headed for Frank's house.

Ana knew that she, along with her brothers and sisters, dad and new mom, would be given a fresh chance at a better life. Arcanja's fresh chance came less than a year after they arrived, when one day she left them for another man. Ana's father fell into despair once again, but he seemed only moderately aggrieved compared to what he experienced after his first wife had died. Ana hoped that Arcanja's departure would be seen as a good omen for a new beginning. She couldn't know whether her dad shared this sentiment.

❧❦

The city streets filled with a flood of steel: big boat-like trucks and cars carrying grownups and crying babies, small box-shaped buildings and large two-story offices squatting like big brick animals on every street. The architecture sat perched in neat rows, structures ready for hunters of all skill levels to attack and carry off its provisions of dry goods, foodstuffs and gifts for loved ones.

Ana was astounded by how many sights, sounds and smells the city offered. She quickly got accustomed to the everyday rainbow of colors, colors that differed greatly from the primary hues she knew from the farm. Those colors had emanated from local vegetation, livestock and free-range chicken—and the same reddish soil that was merely sprinkled throughout São Paulo. Ana's brother had already registered her and the other kids for school. That first day scared them and they cried. Afraid they would be separated for the entire year, they soon learned to cope with the big city's pecking system, where ages and scholastic achievements affected how kids were grouped, typically fifty or more to a class.

In school, the kids were teased mercilessly for their northern accents, their secondhand clothes and their simple lunches, which featured cassava in nearly every dish (porridge, cooked beef or mashed cassava). Ana wished she had someone to turn to. She rarely spoke up and probably wouldn't know what to say if an adult had asked her a simple question. Even hearing, "How is everything going so far" created an uneasy fear.

Ana's stepmom had abandoned them about eight months into the school year. Ana didn't dare add to her dad's burdens with what she thought would be seen as her petty complaints about the bullying, so she daydreamed more and more of the farm, the river, the animals that she once tended like her own brood of smiling babies. The young girl took comfort in the growing realization that her puberty brought with it unexpected benefits. Her budding beauty and womanly stature added confidence to her quiet serenity. She had increasingly learned to accept that her problems were *hers* alone. This too was a mark of growing maturity, along with dealing with the unexpected crisis that erupted without warning.

Ana's thirteenth birthday came and went; there were no gifts or cheerful acknowledgments. Stoically she carried on, trying to help her huge family however she could, but also trying her hardest just to stay caught up in school. Her life revolved around school but no matter how hard it seemed she studied, she was always one step or two behind. Because of her academic lag, she was required to attend Saturday classes as well. One day, just a few months into the official start of the school year, after another grueling six-day week, Ana returned home to find everyone crying.

The shock was immediate: her dad had suffered a stroke and died. First the stepmom had disappeared and now their father was gone.

Ana was orphaned at thirteen and a full-time wage earner a year later. After the funeral the coterie of older brothers and sisters sat the younger kids down to talk about what to do next. They decided to stay in the city and the older kids would take care of the younger kids. Frank, the oldest brother, was engaged, with a wedding planned in the coming months, and another older brother was in a deepening relationship with a girl whose parents had gotten him a decent place to stay. It was clear he was headed down the church aisle soon.

Their father had been the glue that had held them all together, but now it would fall on Ana to leave school and take a sewing job at a factory, so she could help keep the family from tearing apart at its seams.

Besides, she thought, *I know I can enroll for the night school and finish my certificate … That's what Mamãe and Papai would want me to do.*

The other kids got jobs too, some in stores and some as seamstresses, like Ana, in the factory. The two youngest boys stayed in school. It was doubtful if the one, the boy who still suffered seizures, would ever be able to work.

To survive, the kids would parent the other kids. It wouldn't be easy. No longer able to pay rent on the big house, the five younger kids moved into a one-bedroom house outside the city, and took turns caring for the epileptic brother—while the older kids went their own way, getting married within a year or two.

During this time, São Paulo's manufacturing base enjoyed a booming economy that provided laborers like Ana and her sister a lot of overtime. This income allowed the two older girls to support the rest of their family, but the seizures of the one brother became more severe. Many times Ana would get a message at work that her brother was convulsing on the streets and she would run to help.

After sticking a pencil between his teeth for him to bite on, she waited until the episode passed. Then she'd prop him over her shoulders and drag him, and her aching body, back to their house. Once inside, she would change him out of the soaked-through pants he had peed in. She would exchange her stained blouse for a clean one. As much as Ana wished she could finish her studies, her constant mothering of the brother who she took care of would keep her from her dream.

Although the kids were young and without parents, their mutual love and respect kept them committed to a straight and narrow path. None of them drank alcohol, smoked, got into prostitution or anchored themselves to clubs that littered sections of the city. Extremely disciplined, their earlier hardships had prepared them well for this marathon race of survival; and although their mom and dad were gone, their parents' teachings had not departed from their thinking. It helped greatly that the two brothers, now with wives of their own, took the father's place. The older siblings lived on the same street as the youngest of their clan, and they supervised and assisted where they could.

ಌ ✼ ಎ

Not too long after Ana started working, she met a boy. This was the boy who had also come to São Paulo atop the parrot's perch truck. This was the boy who had run screaming to his mother after seeing his father fall down dead in the rain-soaked street.

Ana was fourteen when she and Joseph first locked eyes. She had been a passenger on his bus for a while before she saw his gazelle-like hazel eyes peer at her. She was up hours before the sun, and stood at the same stop to board the 5 a.m. bus downtown, the bus that Joseph captained through the swirl of streets. As soon as she stepped off for her factory seamstress job, her mind knew only the responsibilities attending her: keeping up with production, hungering for the short lunch break that never came soon enough and the sudden call that her brother was in a city square convulsing.

Maybe because of those pressures, ones she managed with little real help from others, she found her thoughts return to that handsome bus driver who obviously liked to look at her. She wanted to let herself be courted by this "boy" who was ten years older.

But Ana was too busy for boys; she worked all day for a boss (and paycheck), worked the evening for her brothers (cooking, helping with schoolwork, then ready for bed) and *then* the rest of the night—attending classes and completing assignments—before she could snatch four hours of sleep from the predawn day.

So, after one year of courting they broke things off and did not "date" again for the next two years. (Her brothers, troubled that Joseph was ten years Ana's senior, did not approve of their courtship, but allowed it—as long as the two of them never went anywhere by themselves. Perhaps having a brother as her social-relationship shadow factored into her decision to end it.)

Two years later when Ana and this bus driving "boy" ran into each other at a wedding, the embers that had died were relit. The relationship that got drenched in a bucket of daily doldrums sparked with new flames.

Although still preoccupied with work, family and school, Ana's seasoned maturity into a well-reasoned woman (well beyond her years) made clear she was ready to pursue an authentic love relationship … on *her* terms.

I am not getting married before finishing school. Do you understand me?

Joseph was so smitten with her he supposed he would have waited till retirement. Love is patient, love is kind and for Joseph, for Ana's kind of love he would be patient. From the day they first met to the day the couple joined as one, nearly ten years had snuck away. But the day of betrothal came, when Joseph asked for the hand of his beautiful bride Ana, who had turned twenty-four only weeks before. With her husband, Ana left the church a happy woman; Joseph left a handsomely rewarded man.

Ana and Joseph on their wedding day,
São Paulo, Brazil, 1962

They had both lived in São Paulo for several years and neither had well-paying jobs. Their financial resources were scarce and just ten months after their wedding they had another mouth to feed. Eleven months later came a second baby, a boy.

Six months after that second baby arrived, Joseph lost his job and Ana, suspecting she was pregnant with a third child, grew increasingly anxious. Although desperate for full-time work, a drought of jobs had hit. Ana's seamstress skills making clothes for neighbors helped pay some of the bills, but the money wasn't enough to support their growing family.

Maybe I'm not pregnant ... only tired from all this stress ... affecting my cycle ... nothing to get excited about. Ana confided in a neighbor, a woman she shared many things with—family matters, men's ways—about her suspicions she might be pregnant a third time.

"You must check very soon, Ana!" the woman told her. "If you are with child it is not too late for you to get what you need. Trust me; this is the best thing to," she said. "There are no jobs anywhere in the country. How will you feed another mouth if your man does not have a job? You are not the first to have an abortion."

Abortion? You mean destroy the life of my baby? How can I do that?

Ana didn't know what to think.

Ana's Journey

She had not heard the word abortion before her neighbor friend said it. Ana and Joseph lived in a small inner-city village. Their modest rented house, one of dozens in nondescript rows, were languid lizards of painted brick and mortar that snaked below the baking São Paulo sun. The front and back yard held no grass or flowering plants. Their small blockhouse, bordered in front and back by sidewalk rectangles of concrete, accentuated the rigid fiscal constraints within which they had to sustain themselves. This had not changed since the day they had gotten married.

They had no TV or appliances to sell for quick cash (or to reduce their monthly utility bills) and the two young parents felt trapped and lost, like a *tartaruga* (turtle) being squeezed from its home.

Ana would have gone back to work in a heartbeat if it weren't for her two little diapered heartbeats that kept her tied to the familial home front. Plus another was on the way. Put plainly, if no jobs existed for a man, there wouldn't have been any for her.

They had already found the most affordable house to live in; so there were no more expenses to cut. *Why did these things always happen at the worst possible moment? Losing his job now,* thought Ana, *is absolutely horrible. Maybe I should get the abortion.* Her female neighbors told her that an abortion was a normal procedure to get rid of an unwanted baby and that a lot of women got abortions. They were quick, not that expensive (a lot cheaper than feeding a baby for the next fifteen years) so she would be stupid not to accept this as a good option.

At first, Ana could not conceive of abortion being a *good* idea. *It is a horrible idea,* she thought, while watching her two little ones play on the floor. Seeing them, she would pat her tummy, knowing that another human being would soon grow to the point of no return.

But this time she convinced herself it was different. Yes, it was a child, just like the ones previously born.

But this is a child we can't afford! It would be wrong *to bring this baby into the world if we can't feed it. Maybe the 'blessing' is to get rid of it now before it gets any bigger. I'm sure it won't feel any pain … It's just a fetus … not a real baby.*

But how could this loving mother of two make such an awful decision? Could she live with the pain and shame of cutting short the blessings for this unborn baby that the other "born babies" had had?

How would I explain this to the kids if they ever ask? Isn't life sacred? Sacrifice a life because Joseph can't find a job? How can my friend Maria give me such advice? Her advice is so cruel yet I know she wants to help…

Ana was also concerned with what her husband would think. But the truth was that Joseph was so focused on finding another job that he forgot about his wife being pregnant again ... so it really was *her* decision to make.

Would the baby live ... or would she help her husband by avoiding the burden of another mouth to feed?

The morning sickness ended like clockwork, just as she mentally crossed off on her calendar the four months that had passed since her last period; and the belly bump had begun to "bump" against the plain *vestido* (dress) she wore. If she delayed her decision any longer, it would be made for her. So, Ana the farmer looked out at her field to survey its yield, knowing that some crops could not be harvested in time for market. Ana decided to let this third tiny field lie fallow.

The next step was cultivating her friend's connections to get the right person to do the abortion. She had already confided to her friend that she *suspected* she might be pregnant, but that was weeks earlier and they had had little contact since. So neither this friend nor any other of Ana's women friends had confirmed that she was with child.

Taking this next fateful step carried risks. Performing an abortion was outlawed in Brazil and pregnancy terminations were done in small homes situated in the backyards of bigger homes. This kept the covert nature of what the women did hidden from nosy neighbors and passers-by. None of the neighborhood women knew she was pregnant and Ana wanted to keep it that way.

The self-taught abortionists (who doubled as area midwives) used crochet needles to puncture the placenta and utilized stomach cancer pills or herbal mixes as potent supplements to be sure the fetus was discharged. The same maternal tools that crafted baby socks and sweaters would, in the abortionists' hands—and in their minds—serve as silver stakes driven through the heart of this unwanted "blob" of tissue.

The house was not far from Ana's own and she was told the midwife was good and worked fast. Now that she had taken that first critical step—she knew the procedure was within reach—Ana stalled. Doubt surged within her.

A few days later, her husband Joseph returned home after a long day standing on the unemployment line … still no jobs. He told her of the country's dire economic situation and that he would probably be unemployed for months, if not a whole year. Soon they would exhaust their savings, so clearly no money could be had for another child. Though he never uttered the words, *Ana, you must get the abortion,* the message conveyed rang loud and clear.

Ana cried into the night. As her sobs passed into spurts of fitful sleep, she faced what seemed a solid wall made of water.

She saw a baby's face staring at her ... mouthing words she could not understand ... she saw a bottle, dropped beside the bobbing head of this quivering torso ... Mamãe, please ... don't ... I want to live.

These words she heard ... through the pool that waded between them ... The bottle turned upright and floated to within reach of the little boy's webbed hands, to suckle life-giving elixir ... but ... a long spear, then another, shot through the watery wall ... piercing his side ... slicing into his body ... cutting off the unformed fingers ... lacerating loose limbs and delicate organs ... then the bottle settled down again, gently, toward the bottom of an aqueous wall ... built like a tomb ... that now dissipated into a vaporous mirage.

"Ana, wake up!"

At first she didn't even recognize her own husband's voice.

"Wake up," he said. "Honey, are you all right? ("Amor, voce está bem?")

Her sobs had sputtered into a series of whimpers and though at first she held the vague image of a bottle of some kind before her eyes, Joseph's gentle but jarring shaking of her shoulders brought her fully awake and aware again of the desperation she was facing. There were no more dreamy images floating in front of her now, only the sobering cold-hard truth that fully submerged her in the crisis pregnancy she was quickly drowning in.

In Brazil then, crisis pregnancy centers didn't exist, but the crisis had engulfed her just the same. There seemed a mass of cells clutching onto her soul and creating the emotional chaos that wouldn't let go. She could not deny it; she wanted the baby, this extra mouth to feed, but also knew that minus the resources and support of her husband she could not keep what she did not want to lose.

Maybe I should tell Carmen and Jandira?

But Ana's sisters had recently married and had their own struggles to contend with. She would be a fool to think they could help much, if at all, with her increasingly cataclysmic situation.

Counseling centers to help women confronting these circumstances did not exist. Family support and financial resources were limited, and Ana felt utterly alone in her heart-wrenching decision.

The next day it seemed the sun had sunk behind an opaque wall of darkened gloom. As she stood under an arch in the courtyard of their building, seeing that the sky forecasted heavy storms, she remembered eerily the day her mom had died. With the ghost of her mom's spirit on her shoulders, Ana decided—grudgingly—that she would get the abortion.

Just as her mother never truly left her, this baby would not always be tethered to her heart. Was a dead baby any less a baby? Though the umbilical cord is cut at birth, isn't an even stronger bond created?

It would be the same with this baby, thought Ana. These slippery slopes of logic allowed her to contain the tears. But her eyes had become her heart ... and not even the cliffs of Mount Roraima could stop the overflow of her despair.

Ana left the kids with a friend and said she had a doctor's appointment, which she said would take a while. The covert clinic was housed in a dark and grimy one-story structure built in the backyard of a grand, splendidly crafted house. This too reminded her of the family's farmhouse the day her mother breathed her last. This city house sprouted a few tawdry stems stuck into the ceiling, with bare bulbs hanging lifeless. Flowering buds designed to shine, but dull as a buried bone. With the curtain of clouds hanging over the house, all light seemed to have been smothered from the room Ana entered that morning. This made it easy for Ana and the woman to avoid looking at each other.

Before Ana fully appreciated how vulnerable she was, she had disrobed and changed into the threadbare gown she was handed, her legs were then pushed apart as helpers leaned her back against a cold slab surface.

A charcoal cloth infused with strong musty odors was held against her privates.

"Breathe slowly Querida, you need to relax," the woman told her. "It will be fine; everything will be all right."

But the sensation felt like ice crystals slashing her skin.

"You will not feel too much more than a little sting," the eyeless woman said.

The coldness spread like thickening ice against her inner thighs and seemed to infiltrate her innards.

"*Oh, you must calm yourself,*" the woman said, louder now. "*Or you will wiggle too much.*"

Ana winced in pain.

"*We are helping you, Senhora.*"

The cavity enclosing her heart now fell numb. Yet she breathed. Exhaling in anxious spurts Ana was a mother possum in a jaguar's mouth.

"Missus, we are almost one. Everything will be good again."

As the women attempted to handle her gingerly, to a point, she could see another woman, Ana's age, limping from an adjacent area with her head hung down. She was ignored by these same women who had attended to her every need minutes before. Oddly, Ana's face resembled her own mother's on the day her mother delivered the baby—the baby that united with his mother in death only days later.

How could everything be good again?

Ana remembered her job as a seamstress on an assembly line. Furiously stitching to meet the day's quota. She was that section of cloth. Worked on piece-meal, a job that had to be finished quickly so the women could get onto the next.

"Here Senhora, take this," the woman said.

The pill she was given was misshapen, not quite round or oval. More like a small blob of chalk.

"Go on, swallow it. This will start the contractions."

She was glad it tasted worse than anything she had put in her mouth. At least one part of her would suffer. And even that was nothing compared to what her baby would endure.

The pale white, dirty walls seemed to lean in over her.

Are you sure you want to do this, Ana? Her thoughts began to chase her.

She closed her eyes and saw her kids. She felt how strong was her urge to love them. There was nothing she wouldn't do for them, and yet for this one, the child who she had never seen or kissed …

We will watch this child for you, Ana. But you will bear the pain.

The walls had turned to waves and now crashed over her. She cried in heaving stabs of anguish, knowing this decision would kill a part of her too.

How many women have lain on this table? How many babies have been sacrificed in this room?

Is this what freedom is? Liberation? Women's rights?

Sometimes, Ana reasoned, one's focus becomes better only after one's reality has been crushed. Ana's ordered life had been crushed under the weight of oppressive "contingencies" and this experience made her see straight. But it was too late.

She had stripped her heart naked. Its moral fibers fallen loosely on the floor, along with her threadbare clothes. Garments that had wrapped her body like a mother's embrace only moments before.

The procedure started. Ana wanted to say sorry to her baby, sorry for keeping him from ever seeing a sun's ray fall upon his pretty hands ... from ever gazing at a blue moon held above the clouds like a baby's toy suspended above the earth's crib ... from ever twinkling upon a star.

Sorry, my baby... I am sorry for taking away from you the chance to be a man or woman, to go to school, to get a degree, to hold a job, to love someone ...

It was too much. The idea that he would never have the option, like she or Joseph had, to build a family, make love, provide love to those she loved, to face life's uncertainties and overcome life's obstacles like she, like they, had done. To conquer fears and achieve or make dreams real.

I wish you could know the reason I had to make this decision. You would understand, wouldn't you?

We couldn't afford to bring you home. You would not have the things you deserve. You understand, don't you?

Then again, maybe not. How could a living being *ever* understand why being killed was better? (Does the fly stay put if it knows it's about to be swatted?) Why would a human life want to die without having first tasted life outside the womb? But there was only one person able to make this life or death decision.

Thoughts paraded through Ana's mind as the misguided ringmaster poked her uterus with a long metal device. Though painful, the onerous task of ejecting this baby from her body loomed larger.

Ana's Journey

This is going to hurt a little, Senhora, but the pain will soon go away. Take this aspirin ... and the lady-killer kept at it, working like a dentist on Ana's exposed cavity. Only this cavity would not be filled, but emptied. *Finally, we're done.*

The abortionist explained to Ana that the baby was bigger than she had expected and that the fetal parts would come out slowly over the next few days.

You can expect heavy bleeding, Senhora ... and some tenderness for a while. You look so sad; don't feel bad. It is not a baby, just a blob of tissue, like a tumor.

Rest, Senhora ... here on the couch.

Ana lay back on that cracked leather couch for an hour before going back home.

The minutes passed like a two-ton clock ticking on her chest. But the guilt of what she had done weighed heavier. When she finally rose, her eyes spent with tears, she knew the life she had crushed suffered more than the adult heart that sat crumpled inside her.

She looked back and saw the house shrink as the bus pulled away. *WAIT!* she wanted to scream. *Stop the bus ... I left my baby at that house!*

But Ana bit her tongue. She did what she did and now there was no turning back. In fact, she didn't want to ever get off that bus. She wished it would keep going, taking her farther and farther from the place she had committed her worst-ever atrocity. An act so low she couldn't fathom how she'd pull herself back up. Inside the bus, movement dominated.

People got on and off, young women cuddled and softly rocked their babies, older men spoke in animated arcs, their arms flung here and there, while kids reached innocently for treats nestled in dusty pockets and bags. The ebb of life prevailed around Ana's orb, but inside she knew death had vanquished a life.

Her tummy never got a chance to look pregnant, but it used to be hard and firm. Now it was flabby. Still big, but lifeless. No more baby moving inside.

The kicks that she felt for never came. The kicks that she missed. A lot of kicks hit her uterine walls during the procedure. That little prizefighter fighting for the prize of his life but his feet and fists fell quiet. There was no doubt the baby was gone.

She barely made it home and fell into the couch as if it were an airtight casket. Dizzy, weak and wan, Ana could feel the profuse bleeding continue inside her. Unconcerned with her own frail and anemic condition, she couldn't stop thinking about what she had just done.

How could I betray my own child? I raised my brothers and sisters under much worse circumstances. Why didn't I wait? Maybe Joseph would get a job? And everything would be fine again. Why? Why, why?

Sullenness and sleep forced her eyes shut and soon she stood at the edge of a field. Warm winds whirled from the hidden trees, but from the underbrush she could see the outline of an older woman cupping an almost dead bird in her hand ... telling her the bird had almost been killed.

Ana's Journey

A tiny pip chirped from its beak, but then its head dropped into the cusp of the woman's hand and closed its eyes.

She awoke with a veil of lachrymose lace and slumped to her knees, with the words of the Lord's prayer escaping her lips, she begged God to forgive her.

My Father in heaven, your will be done ... but PLEASE, Almighty God, give me a second chance!

She could hear the echo of the abortionist's words—*Senhora, your baby is gone*—but Ana had faith that there might yet be a wee life left untouched. Protected by the Almighty God that she now implored, *Please don't let my baby die.*

The abortionist had warned her not to worry because it would take days for the whole *sujeira*, or blob, to come out. She bled all night and like the doctor illegitimate said, many pieces of the "sujeira" blob had come out with the blood. Two days later Ana again prayed for her Father in heaven to forgive her sins committed against her baby. Ultrasound machines had been invented but they were not available where Ana lived. There was no way to know for sure if God had answered her pleas. The abortionists were doctors of death and were very successful in terminating pregnancies, so Ana struggled to believe that her baby wasn't also dead. But she had heard cases of aborted fetuses surviving.

A month passed and her abdomen had not flattened; it was instead becoming taut as before and, incredulously, she was gaining weight. Then, on a cool but sunny day in March, when a mild breeze kicked up a white, washed sheet that Ana had pinned to the clothesline—she felt a tepid tap. Had she eaten something spicy that caused her stomach to gurgle?

It can't be the baby, Ana thought. *It has been almost a month since the procedure.*

Although she had continued to pray for a miracle, she figured it was a lost cause. Her own selfishness had caused it and God was letting her suffer for her sinful choice.

But, what if...

She quickly let the damp towels tumble into the hamper so she could lie down next to the walled well on the sun-warmed grass. This time she placed her hand on her tummy with a feeling of disbelief tinged with happy hopefulness.

Could the baby really be alive?

The fourth week since the procedure had come and gone, with the bleeding all but gone and yet it seemed like a life continued to grow inside her. She turned to look at the wicker basket; she could see the white sheets and dress she wore when she learned she was pregnant. Was it white or black? She couldn't tell with the way the straw shaded the sun's rays. Had she allowed her faith to fade in the shadows of God's own Son? Had she locked the Lord's Son by the clouds of her unbelief?

Later that day, while lying on the worn leather couch, a green that matched the patches of sod outside, she reached for a snack that her one-year-old clamored for. That's when she felt the unmistakable kick of a little baby.

She popped another *rapadura* (molasses and sugar-cane candy) in her mouth and again ... a baby's kick! She cried out in joy and fear.

The baby wasn't gone ... the baby had just signaled that a life still grew inside. Joy-tears lined her face. She knew that God, the eternal Author of eternal life, had interceded to give her this second glorious chance. He hadn't let her baby die.

But how would she tell Joseph? The possibility of deformity also settled upon her concerns. That night she asked Joseph to put his ear over her tummy and tell her what he heard. He told her he heard what sounded like a heartbeat, but he wasn't sure if it was hers or a baby's. She was dumbfounded and Joseph was struck just plain dumb, without a word to offer.

She could tell he didn't know what to think or what to say. They had spent almost all their money on the abortion—to *save* money—and now after the money was gone, the baby wasn't?

I am sorry, Amor. This is my fault.

How could she explain it to him? How could she share all the emotions tugging at her heart?

I have prayed to God to save our baby. Even as I lay on that table as they stabbed ... I couldn't believe how I could let that happen. After I left I cried so much and started to beg our Father in heaven to make my mistake go away. It's my fault, Amor, it's all my fault.

Ana had always believed in the sanctity of human life and here she was trying to pacify her hardworking husband's worst fears by *apologizing* for *wanting* their baby to live she was baffled by the ludicrousness of her own hypocrisy.

Thankfully, he didn't say a word and went to sleep. She was wide awake all night, a Friday. The last few days she had prayed over the same verse from Psalm 139 and now she found herself repeating it as some kind of divine prophecy.

For You formed my inward parts, you covered me in my mother's womb.

Maybe, Ana thought, this would be a "church-approved" charm to prod the baby to move, to reestablish contact with that tenacious tiny thing. On Monday morning she went to see her gynecologist, who she had not uttered a word to of her humiliating disappointment in getting an abortion. But to remove any suspicion he might have had, she told him there had been some bleeding.

He checked her vital signs, inspected her, then placed the stethoscope against her lower abdomen (where the baby, if there was one, would be curled in the placenta) and listened. The forty seconds seemed like forty days, but at the end of this exodus, Ana heard the physician's whispered, "divine" words as if transfused from God Himself: *Your baby's heart sounds good.* Ana wanted to burst into screams. She wanted to jump from the examination table onto the wall, and fall at the doctor's feet—but she did nothing. She hid the failed abortion from everyone and buried it in her heart. It would remain a venal secret she would take to the grave … (or so she thought).

After seven sevens, or forty-nine days, since the botched abortion, Ana's husband landed a truck-driving job for a big, Brazilian transit company. The insurmountable fear of not having enough money for another baby had been surmounted. The molehill that Joseph and Ana's anxieties had made into a mountain, God had reduced to an impotent pile of rubble.

As the months slid by, Ana's due date fast approached. Although thrilled the baby's miraculous life had been confirmed, she worried there would be deformities.

Considering the amount of blood lost when the embryonic effluvia had exited her birth canal, she assumed the extent of the damage caused to her baby would be considerable. She focused on the answer to her prayers, that despite her attempt to end its life, the baby had after all survived. So the question of whether he (or she) would be born whole or disfigured seemed secondary.

The August 12 due date came and went, but still no baby had arrived. Ultrasound machines had been invented a few years before, but none were yet available for Ana's town. The hours ticked by like days, the days stretched like weeks with the frigid temperatures doing nothing to cool Ana's rising impatience.

Finally, on August 30, 1964, her water broke and a very enlarged Ana was taken to the hospital. Because she had developed gestational diabetes (common in many pregnancies) the doctors could not perform a Cesarean section delivery. They tried to induce labor but failed, so Ana was carted on a gurney to the intensive care unit (ICU) to await the next step. She couldn't talk or move due to her condition and medicine they had given her, but Ana was very aware of her situation. She was cognizant of being in the hospital give birth to a baby that would likely be mutilated or mentally handicapped. Those deficiencies did not alter one iota the love she carried inside.

She ached to hold him in her arms and carry him home like a king to his castle ... if a girl, then as a queen after her coronation.

Joseph, who had waited with growing anxiousness, now needed a helping hand with the predicament he was in. With Ana ready to have their third baby, and two small ones at home, he couldn't watch the children, take care of Ana, and work all day. He phoned several of Ana's sisters and brothers and soon they all knew that Ana was hospitalized and in the ICU due to complications with the pregnancy. But Joseph turned to Carmen, the sister who shared the same house. One of Ana's brothers, serving in the military, was stationed three hours away; and, sadly, the enfeebled brother who suffered epileptic fits had died after a horrible seizure on the very day

Ana delivered her first baby. Carmen was Ana's only sibling still in the area, so Joseph called her first.

He contacted the church where Carmen and the orchestra were rehearsing and when she was told her brother-in-law's message, that Ana might be in critical condition, Carmen's thoughts turned immediately to the day their mother had died, from post-delivery complications. *This would be Ana's fate, too,* she thought, before collapsing into sobs. After the conductor asked why she was crying he spontaneously canceled the rehearsal. The conductor and some of Carmen's church friends accompanied her to the hospital to visit Ana. Once there, they saw Ana crying. She had sworn herself to secrecy. She didn't say a word about the abortion, but shared that something was wrong with the baby and the doctor told her she couldn't have a C-section.

The choirmaster spoke up. *Ana, can I pray for you?* She consented. Then he asked, *Could I read a scripture to you?* She said yes again. He prayed for her and her baby's health, for God's hand upon the doctors and then he read from the Bible (John 3:16): *"For God so loved the world that He gave His only begotten Son, that whosoever believes in Him shall not perish but have eternal life."*

Although she had considered herself a devout Catholic her whole life, Ana did not remember reading that verse ever before. She believed in Him, and she didn't want to perish, but when the conductor asked her if she would like to give her life to Christ and accept His death as atonement for her sins, it felt strange to say yes, because she thought that was something non-Catholics or non-Christians did.

But she could not hide from God her abortion secret, neither could she cover up her other unconfessed sins. It made sense, therefore, that she understand and acquiesce to the one person who already knew her secret sin. Because now she was reminded very clearly that it was He who could, and would, forgive her for trying to destroy the baby that was, ultimately, *His* creation. Three hours later, Ana delivered a 9.8-pound baby boy. Her son, who she named John, to honor the Bible verse, was born just one hour into the new day on August 31.

As if his birth hadn't been miraculous enough, the baby's body was delivered intact, with no detached or lacerated limbs, nor amputated fingers or toes. He was as big and beautiful a newborn as either of Ana's other two. When the doctor brought him out, he handed Ana her baby, who steered his mouth straight to her breast for milk. While enjoying his first suckling from his mama's breast, his little beads of eyes surveyed her face as carefully as an explorer looking down at a map in search of treasure.

She looked at him in awe and marveled, *Is it possible he's already trying to tell me something?* And though she knew a brand-new baby could not yet reason, it really did seem he was talking, using thought words, saying, *It is so nice meeting you finally ... thank you, Mamãe, for keeping me.*

That mother, who stared into her baby's eyes, was my mother. That almost-aborted baby was my younger brother. She told me the story of her secret abortion attempt when I was twelve. She trusted me, her firstborn, with this "skeleton in a closet" after I promised I would not let it out. I was not to tell John until after she was gone from this earth. She was so ashamed of what she had done and agonized over John's reaction if he were ever to find out.

Twenty-two years later, one month after her death, John was in Chicago visiting me from Brazil. Of course by this time he was all grown and had begun attending law school in São Paulo.

I was sautéing thick slices of butternut squash on the stove. This vegetable was a favorite of his and we were enjoying the creamy fresh aromas on an October afternoon, giggling and telling stories of our childhood, about our mom's sense of humor, her impetuous laugh, timid smile and puritanical ways. Mostly, of how much we missed having her around. Maybe it was easier with him half hidden fixing a pipe under my sink, but the moment took me back to ...

Ina, you have to promise me——That you will NEVER *speak of this to anyone ... not ANYONE ... until I am gone. You understand me? (Yes, Mamãe. I promise. What can't I tell anyone?)*

Before John was born, I made a very bad ... I made a very bad decision, that I kept to myself. I never told a soul. Only God knows.

As I stood there, over the big pan sizzling with home cooking, my brother's legs sticking out from the cabinet like a half-born calf, the misty tears welled up like I remember my mother's tears formed. As I recalled her telling me her secret, I remembered how she had cried and laughed with equal measure: tortured by the death she had nearly caused, but also exuberant by how God's hand blessed in bringing her condemned baby son back from the dead.

"John," I said. "Did you know there was a secret that mom told me that I promised never to tell you until after she was gone?"

I turned the flame low, added crystals of salt and crushed pepper, and narrated the story just as I remembered it from my mother's mouth. John's wrench went silent as I spoke. It seemed an hour but it couldn't have been more than fifteen or twenty minutes. Afterward he stood up and put his hands on the counter gripping the sink. His head dropped low and neither of us said a word. His fierce pride would not let him cry openly in front of his sister though I sensed a slight ripple of muscle move across his shoulders.

Finally, with solemn yet tender eyes, he turned to me, and with a curtain of laced wetness surrounding his eyes asked, *Why didn't you tell me before, Ina? I would have kissed her feet, hugged her and thanked her for keeping me.*

I promised her, John. That's why I'm telling you now.

It's funny Ina, but I always felt deep inside like I had an obligation to please Mom—as if I owed her something I could never repay. But I never knew why.

Now you know, John.

My mom died at age sixty-one and my brothers, dad and uncles were her pallbearers. As John stood at the shoulder side of my mother's casket for the procession to begin, our eyes met and my tears slid from my face like slippery pellets. I thought of my mom, how happy she must have been when she locked eyes with her baby that she had almost killed.

Ana had three more babies after John: Regina, David and Vera. But the throng of poor kids living in the slums of Brazil became her kids too. Every week my mom organized a Sunday school for the ones who had no way to get to church. She led a women's hospital ministry and visited infirm patients every Thursday, people who had no other visitors. She made many friends and often provided the last soothing human voice they heard before falling into their final sleep. But from the perspective of my siblings, and me, our mom was a wondrous cook, an honorable wife and an adoring, unforgettable parent.

My mom, Ana, told me more than once how she had prayed for God to grant her one more mercy when her time came. Not to let her suffer or wither away in a hospital bed. And this plea too came to pass.

On November 9, 1999, Ana was admitted to a São Paulo hospital with a horrible headache. A major blood vessel in the brain had burst, an aneurysm that the doctors did all they could to repair, but their efforts weren't enough. Two days after she was admitted, she called the nurse into her room.

Before Ana died, the nurse who attended to her said, "As I walked toward your mother's bed, she looked at the window as if she could see someone there ... then put on her best smile ever and expired. I have never seen someone before or since die such a beautiful death."

My mother, Anaide (Ana) Alves da Silva led a full and productive life. The same as anyone's life not every moment shone with silver or sparkled like gold. But the full value of how she lived and the choices she chose outweighed the deficits she felt. She was blessed to have been happily married to her husband Joseph for forty-one years and to have seen her children grow to be adults. These are her kids, who meant the world to her: Ina (that's me), Harold, John, Regina and Vera.

On December 29, 2011 Joseph went to be with the Lord. Not one day went by in which he didn't cry for his beloved wife. During his 11 years as a widower, he would still pick up his guitar and sing to Ana while looking up to heaven. Now they are together again. Dad, the one who so passionately told Poli's story to me, lived a very hard but happy life. He died at the age of 83 and up to a month before his death, he was still jogging every morning.

Though I was only twelve when my mom shared her abortion story with me, her experience and intimate confession began to move upon my heart years later, which resulted in my decision to open Crisis Pregnancy Centers in Brazil. At fourteen I gave my life to Christ and began asking the Lord to show me His plans for my life. I tried playing violin and guitar in the church orchestra, but didn't feel the "call," so I kept seeking His will. I took part in the church drama team for a few years, but that wasn't my call either. Then, while in college, I began attending divinity school on weekends, to study Christian theology. I wanted to learn more about the Bible and to find out what God's call was for my life. I was convinced (as I still am) that God has a plan for each person's life, that no one is a mistake. And as far as I was concerned, if God had written out an "Ina plan," I wanted to know exactly what it was while I still had time on this earth.

Ana's Journey

One night, during August, Brazil's winter, when I was nineteen, I dreamt of a place that looked like a disco. It was very dark and full of women crying, wailing and groaning. In my mind I could see them yanking at their hair and all around were walls that spewed flames of fire coming. Screaming in pain, all of these women seemed small from where I stood, atop a tall building. Then someone near—a someone I couldn't see—said, *This is your call, Ina.* I didn't understand it, but then I remembered my mom's testimony that day when I was twelve and all that pain and regret and shame after her abortion came back to me. That was what my dream was about. And I finally accepted the Lord's call upon my life.

I immediately looked for places in Brazil that helped women in similar situations that my mom had faced, but I had no luck. Places to assist women facing a crisis pregnancy did not exist, so I gave up my search. I finished college with a degree in language translation and interpretation, and t hen traveled to the United States to study, where I met the man who I would marry. After getting married, we moved to Chicago, his home city, in January 1993. The very day I arrived in Chicago, I heard a "Hike for Life" promotion on Chicago's biggest Christian radio station. Hike for Life was a way for volunteers to raise money for area crisis pregnancy centers. At that moment the call on my life was reconfirmed. I called the number announced on the radio and got the information I wanted.

Once I started helping these women, I never stopped. I volunteered at the Chicago center for a few years and after my husband and I had two girls, first Rachel and then Rebecca, the Lord called upon me to open a crisis pregnancy center in Brazil, despite serious domestic problems in my marriage. No matter how stressed out I was, the Lord's Holy Spirit would wake me at three o'clock sharp *every night for seven months* and would tell me to open a center in Brazil.

Finally, God clearly directed me to follow the design His call on my life would take. I telephoned Life Pregnancy Center in Grand Rapids, Michigan (USA), the only agency with an international ministry affiliation I knew of, and I asked the manager if she would be interested in opening a Center in Brazil. She asked me if I could go to Grand Rapids for a meeting and the next week I was on a plane. They helped me open that first center, in São Paulo, in May of 2000. Thereafter Brazil4Life operated independently, but I remain grateful to their support in that early stage in the ministry's birth. To date, Brazil4Life, has planted fifteen crisis pregnancy centers in Brazil. We have plans to open Crisis Pregnancy Centers all over Brazil and anywhere in the world the Lord leads us to.

Since that first facility opened in May of 2000, our Brazil4Life crisis pregnancy centers and staff have helped more than 9,000 women choose life for their babies.

"Open your mouth for the speechless, in the cause of all who are appointed to die." – Proverbs 31:8

Brazil4Life International, partnering with International Teams U.S., (http://www.iteams.us/) has opened crisis pregnancy centers in São Paulo, Rio de Janeiro, Niteroi, Belo Horizonte, João Pessoa, Salvador, Venda Nova, Betin, Recife and Angra dos Reis. Each center operates independently, with many connected to local churches. Each center has a board of directors, a team of committed volunteers and a director who receives extensive professional training for this specialized work. Together these teams work tirelessly over many hours, giving of their loving concern and attention to women facing a crisis in their pregnancy. My mother didn't know that telling her story to me would be like a planted flower bulb, lying dormant in my thoughts, but that would one day flower into this little book.

That same seed has germinated in the hearts of many women all across Brazil, who heard a similar call from God to help women in distress. Many of these women now serve as volunteers in the centers planted in Brazil.

Plans exist to open more centers, with discussions to increase assistance for the many unborn and newborn babies and their moms who will need our help. We strive to be a place of refuge for both those facing the hardest decision of bringing forth a new life, and for those who carried out the desperate decision of terminating their baby's life. The guilt and pain of that decision can be grueling and isolating, but we are here to comfort not condemn or criticize. Your purchase of this book helps fund the planting of new crisis pregnancy centers and abstinence programs in Brazil.

We do not act as a judge appointed by the one true God, because we understand that no one is morally superior to another, for according to the Bible, "we all have sinned and fall short of the glory of God."

According to The Center for Bio-Ethical Reform (www.abortionno.org), 115,000 abortions are performed daily in the world, or 4,800 abortions per hour of every day. That represents eighty abortions per minute globally. Each year, this hidden desecration kills about as many Americans as have been killed on all the battlefields of all the wars in U.S. history. One person or one ministry cannot stop abortion or change every person's mind, but we can give those looking for help an alternative that could restore their sense of regret to a sense of purpose and attitude of despair to an attitude of hope.

I have met many women that cringe with disappointment when reflecting on their abortion decision, but I have met no woman who regretted bringing her baby to term and holding that little ball of loving breath.

Brazil4Life provides pro-life speakers for school presentations and youth groups. Topics include alternatives to abortion, and abstinence-until-marriage explanations that other young people share in a very positive, entertaining way. These peers explain their values and the long-term consequences of the decisions that teens make. Teaching these adolescents that choosing abstinence is actually the "in" option also means they will want to avoid the impending crisis of an unwanted pregnancy or a sexually transmitted disease (STD) that their unwise choices could lead to.

Brazil4Life is a not-for-profit organization. To learn more about our work, our volunteers, and how you can help, please visit our website at www.brazil4life.org or email Ina at brazil4lifeintl@gmail.com or isobolewski@msn.com.

To make a charitable contribution, please visit www.iteams.org/us/giving-form. Below "IT/USA Donation," type "brazil4Life" in the first row and follow the instructions or mail your donation to:

Brazil4life/iteams international
411 West River Road
Elgin, IL 60123 USA

To have Ina speak at your church or pro-life gathering, please email isobolewski@msn.com or call her @847 863 2003. Like us on Facebook at brazil4LifeIntl and follow us on Twitter @ brazil4lifeintl.

John, the abortion survivor, with his nieces Rebecca (left) and Rachel, who appear quite happy they have him in their lives.

 Ina was born and raised in São Paulo, Brazil, and as an adolescent learned her mother's intimate secret, one her mother shared, that Ina's younger brother John was nearly aborted. From that awareness of her mother's "deep regret," Ina decided to help other women who faced the effects or after-effects of an unwanted pregnancy. Ina has served as a volunteer for Crisis Pregnancy Centers in the Chicago land since February 1993, promoting the Hike for Life and speaking at many Sanctity of Human Life Month events throughout Chicago and its suburbs. She has been affiliated with International Teams since 2011, and has opened several independently managed Crisis Pregnancy Centers in Brazil with brazil4Life International, a nonprofit she continues to direct. Additionally, she participated in the "Brazil Without

Abortion" campaign in Brazil's capital, Brasilia, and founded a national youth abstinence program that reaches teens with discipline and self-esteem lessons based on having a right relationship with the Lord. Ina's husband of 15 years died in 2007. Ina and her two daughters, Rachel and Rebecca, live in a Chicago suburb.

Ron has reported, written and edited professionally for more than 25 years, for newspapers, magazines, ministries, websites, nonprofit and corporate institutions.